The Battle for Nigeria

By Dalen Garris

This is a work of history. Historical individuals and places and events are mentioned.

For information, address
dale@revivalfire.org

First paperback printing August, 2021

Cover design by Renee Garris

Printed in the United States of America

Epilogue

I stood on a ridge overlooking the valley. It was that time of the day that is half dark – not evening, but more like a shadowy daytime. It felt dreary.

Facing me on the other side of the valley was another ridge similar to the one I was on. It was covered in darkness and thick clouds like a thunderstorm coming over the mountains. I could hear war drums in the distance coming from behind that storm – boom, boom, boom. Like the impending doom and destruction of a coming war.

For some reason, I could not turn my head to the left or the right, but I could see with my peripheral vision a long line of huge white chargers on either side of me stretching as far as I could see. They were stronger and taller than any horse I had ever seen, about 10 feet tall at the bridle. I somehow knew these were the Lord's warhorses and that sitting on every one of them was a strong angel prepared for battle.

As I stood there feeling small and insignificant, a wave passed before us of the white-hot righteousness of Almighty God that took my breath away. I couldn't see Him for the glory of His presence, but I knew this was the Lord of Hosts reviewing His troops.

That valley was Nigeria, and I had to go down into that valley and plant as many seeds of the Gospel as I could before the battle was enjoined.

I did not have much time War was coming to Nigeria.

Contents

Battlefield Nigeria

Then I went on to the gate of the fountain, and to the king's pool: but there was no place for the beast that was under me to pass.

Then went I up in the night by the brook, and viewed the wall, and turned back, and entered by the gate of the valley, and so returned.

... Then said I unto them, Ye see the distress that we are in, how Jerusalem lieth waste, and the gates thereof are burned with fire: come, and let us build up the wall of Jerusalem, that we be no more a reproach.

Then I told them of the hand of my God which was good upon me; as also the king's words that he had spoken unto me. And they said, Let us rise up and build. So they strengthened their hands for this good work.

(Nehemiah 2:14-15, 17-18)

Piercing the Cloud

Nigeria is a very different place. I'm not sure how different it is from the surrounding countries in West Africa, but it sure is a lot different than any of the other places in East Africa that I've been to.

Your first impression when you get off the plane feels slightly out of focus. On the surface, everything seems the same as other African countries, and yet there is something that lies just beneath it that you can't quite put your finger on. It's just different somehow. A somber blanket lies in the air that lends a subdued feeling to everything. There isn't that feeling of color and laughter in the air. It's as if Nigeria has stepped out of Technicolor into a world that is colored in shades of grey. Life is a serious undertaking here.

Is it the culture? Is it just the way it is? Or is it something deeper than that makes everything seem so drab – something deeply spiritual in nature?

I have spent the last two weeks bringing a message of revival to several churches whose hearts are turned to God for something other than the same old stuff that they have been hearing. Something different has to happen.

Their desperation for a true move of God is rising and pushing past the ineffective platitudes and promises of blessings they have been given. It's not working, and they know it. I am embarrassed to say that these messages of false prosperity and unmerited blessings have poured forth from America, and so many innocent people have believed that because America has been so blessed, this message must be true.

By now, however, they are beginning to realize that it's not working. Something is missing. This is not the same gospel that our grandfathers preached and they are not getting the same results. We have forgotten something along the way as we followed the Pied Pipers of Prosperity and Blessings off into a modern Gospel that is softer and more "loving" than that old message of repentance and the fear of God. Our Bible colleges churned out a new generation of pastors and taught them to discard the old God of Judgment for a new God of Love. And in the process, we lost something so vital in the Church that we don't know how to find our way back.

Satan has done such a complete job of turning our focus onto ourselves that we don't even realize how far we have turned from the Cross. The message that I bring is predicated upon the concept that the Gospel of Jesus Christ is not about you – it is about others – and revival will not come until we turn our focus to the lost that are dying in sin.

But no matter how hard I drive this message home, I will often hear another preacher get up right after me and promise the same people all kinds of new blessings, new deliverances, new miracles in their lives ... all for free! And the crowd that had just bowed their heads in recognition of their own self-serving ways will now jump to their feet and cheer as this new preacher promises them all kinds of blessings and negates everything that I just preached. Just human nature, I guess.

Revival is not free -- neither is it cheap -- and breaking through this cloud that covers their Pollyanna Gospel mindset, not only in Nigeria but all across Africa, is essential before any move of God will come. Is this the spiritual cloud I feel here that sucks the life and joy out of the very air? Could it be that Satan has entrenched himself here in Nigeria as his last stand of resistance to stop revival at any cost? Is Nigeria the last bastion of darkness that must be conquered to allow the Great African Revival to break forth?

Many here believe that Nigeria is highly chosen for this great move of God and that is why Satan has concentrated his darkness to destroy this nation. It is not the sinners he must control; it's the Christians. And what better way than to lull them into a false sense of security with a "love gospel" that has worked since he first used it in the Garden of Eden. It's all about you. Don't worry. Hakuna Matata. Thou shalt not surely die because God loves you. Here, take a bite.

There are heroes here in Nigeria. Men and women who are willing to take a stand that will invoke the ire of the Church in an attempt to wake them up. Many will hear the call of the trumpet and rise to the challenge. Many will not, but will resist and attack those who will. Battle lines are forming, choices are being made, and destinies are being decided.

It is a time for war, and Nigeria is the battleground.

"Blow ye the trumpet in Zion, and sound an alarm in my holy mountain: let all the inhabitants of the land tremble: for the day of the LORD cometh, for it is nigh at hand;" (Joel 2:1)

Pure Religion and Undefiled

"Pure religion and undefiled before God and the Father is this, To visit the fatherless and widows in their affliction, and to keep himself unspotted from the world." (James 1:27)

Nigeria is like no other place I have been. As the most populous country in Africa, the pressure of their dense population tends to make them a stronger, more aggressive culture. That is both good and bad – that which is bad is really bad, but that which is good is really good. I saw some of the really good this evening.

The church where I am preaching at for three days is on a campaign to start a true Holy Ghost revival. As the revivalist guest speaker, I am a major part of that plan. I tell them what to do to have revival, and they go out and put it into practice. My goal is that they will grab hold of a vision that will claim their entire community for Christ, and have the faith to believe that they can change the world. And they can ... they just have to have to want it bad enough.

It has to start somewhere, and tonight they started with an open-air crusade. Outdoor crusades do not work well in America - at least as far as I have seen – but they sure work well here in Africa. At the end of the service tonight, at least 50-50 souls came to the altar to get saved. They were plugged into one of the local churches here and were instructed on what to do next in their Christian walk. This is pure religion. It does not get any better, deeper, heavier, or more essential than this.

In contrast, many churches have developed a more layered and sophisticated way of operating. I guess it is only natural given that the Church today has become very much like a corporate business. Aspiring pastors apply for positions at various churches just like a job applicant fresh out of business school. Once hired, salaries are set, job descriptions and responsibilities are defined, and positions are secured. They start as a Youth Pastor (why do we put our most inexperienced clergy in the most sensitive position?) and move on up through the different departments until they arrive at the pinnacle of Senior Pastor. Programs are instituted, goals are voted on, methods are applied, and the whole machinery of church is organized.

This is denominational religion. Like it or not, complain, criticize, or praise it, this is how it is done -- and I suppose it works well enough for what it is supposed to accomplish -- but what I experienced this evening was pure religion. This was raw "go out and get 'em" Christianity -- out in the street, face to face where they live. Nothing complicated. Just do it.

I tell the churches I preach at that if they are sitting in church waiting for souls to come, they will wait forever. They're not coming. You know why? Because they are afraid they will become just like us. (You can always hear everyone groan when I say that). "Go ask them", I tell them, "They will tell you."

What they want is the real thing. They've already heard the message – probably know it better than most "church people" – but they're not interested in what you believe, what you say, or what new fancy programs you have going. They want the real thing – they want to see the power. They don't want the Gospel that is the philosophy of God – defined, analyzed, organized, packaged, and digested in your theological books and scholastic dissertations. They want the Gospel that is the power of God unto Salvation. Raw power; raw truth. And if they don't see it in your church, is it a small wonder why they are not coming?

Proverbs tells us that he that winneth souls is wise. This evening, over fifty people changed their eternal destination and escaped burning in Hell for Eternity. I saw more wisdom in the simple zeal and faith of these people to go out and do this one thing than in all the sophisticated Bible College programs that our modern religions can muster.

I'm sure the scribes will object ... but then, they always have, haven't they?

"Salt is good: but if the salt have lost his savor, wherewith shall it be seasoned? It is neither fit for the land nor yet for the dunghill; but men cast it out.

He that hath ears to hear, let him hear."

(Luke 14:34-35)

Childbirth

It's the eyes that get you.

All the shouting and the praising are great, but it is when you look into their eyes and see the sincerity of their heart that you know that God is doing something special here. It's not just another meeting to sing some songs and hear about how much God wants to bless you and bring you into some vaunted abundant life. The stuff we saw tonight is down to the roots of the soul – serious dedication to do whatever it takes to have revival.

Nigeria is very different from East Africa in that this is a serious people. You do not see the color and gaiety here that you find in Kenya, but neither do you see the lackadaisical attitude that you find in East Africa. Nigerians work hard and have a more serious outlook on life.

Their approach to the Gospel reflects that same attitude. Whereas in Kenya, the shouting and singing may be louder initially, their ardor begins to wane when it comes time to dig in and do the work of the Gospel. Nigerians, on the other hand, may not be so open and emotional, but they seem to have a more serious fixation on the hard facts of the price that must be paid to have a true revival.

A prominent pastor here told me that they have been fasting and praying for revival but God is not answering. Something is wrong, and they want to know what it is. Now that is a serious cry for revival! This is past the singing and dancing and enters into the serious reality of what God requires. The Altar of God is not a place of singing and dancing, but of blood and sacrifice and death.

One of the biggest lies that Satan has sold the Church is that we can just sit in our little pews and God will have mercy on us and send us revival. Sorry, but if you do nothing, nothing will happen. Mercy is not handed out free – it must be paid for. Mercy begets mercy, unto the merciful He will show Himself merciful, and as James tells us, judgment shall be without mercy on those who have shown no mercy. What a trip the devil has put us on! And we believed him! Or should that be in the present tense?

But these guys know differently. They know there is a price to pay for everything in God – everything. And the price for a full Holy Ghost revival is extremely high. That's why they are so rare – nobody wants to pay that price. That is precisely why you have to be desperate to see revival come. So desperate that you are like Rachael in Genesis 30:1, "Give me souls or else I will die!" So desperate that you are willing to give your life so that souls can be saved. If you are not, you will not see a real Holy Ghost revival because you won't do what it takes to get one. You'll just have some really good "church".

But these people tonight have had enough of "church". They are ready for whatever God has placed before them and are ready to answer the call of the trumpet that is blowing in Zion – the call to the last battle between God and Satan for the souls of Man.

You could see it in their eyes as they came in droves to kneel at the altar. The entire church came down -- even the ushers! They emptied themselves of their self-interest and pride as they ripped their hearts wide open to repent and surrender all to Jesus. The passion at the altar was only surpassed by the cries of "hallelujah" that were so loud that my ears over-amped! There was victory in the church tonight.

When you see a serious dedication like that, you can expect serious results. I have no doubt that their passion will carry them into the Word of God to give them the power to fast and pray for God to build a fire in their church. And then watch as that fire spills out into the streets to bring in the lost and dying into that same Holy Ghost blaze.

Just as in childbirth, revivals are birthed in pain and labor and travail. They also end up with the same kind of rejoicing.

Nigerian Pharisees

Nigeria has been hard. I knew there would be a battle, but I didn't expect the intensity of what we have faced here. But it is in the thick smoke of battle that warriors are forged, and I expect we will see God raise up a crop of serious Christians who, because they were born in adversity, will rise to the challenge He has placed before them. I just hope I'm not one of them, because I'm getting tired in my old age.

Beyond the accompanying physical troubles and afflictions that I and those who are with me have faced here, the greatest challenge Nigeria faces is to be able to pierce through the smoke of satanic deception. The real enemy to be concerned with is not the Muslim extremists or any of the sinners – it is the Church.

What's new? Christianity's perpetual enemy has always been the organized "ecclesiastical powers that be". Who sold Joseph into slavery? Who chased David in the wilderness? Who delivered Jesus to be crucified? Who slaughtered millions of Christians throughout the Middle Ages? What is this deep animosity that possesses the soul of the Church once it becomes entrenched into society? Within a few generations, a moment that was once birthed in persecution often becomes the persecutor.

As you walk down any street in Nigeria, even out in the rural villages, you can count the churches lining up every few hundred yards or so. You may have three and four of them in the same building! Posters are everywhere proclaiming the showers of blessings, a night of miracles, and your time of deliverance if you will just come to their meeting.

If you rise up to expose these lies, you are threatening the very existence of these preachers who have sucked the fat out of these poor people, and they will work tirelessly to stop you. In the same way, Jesus threatened the power of the Pharisees when He preached about repentance and took away their power of Levitical judgment. And they killed Him for it.

Satan knows that no revival will come without repentance, and that is where he must draw his battle lines. He is armed with a myriad of lies that have worked for 6,000 years and his polished talents as the world's smoothest liar. We, on the other hand, are armed with the Word of God, but we need courage to swing that sword in battle. Sounds easy, but come to Nigeria and start exposing these lies of prosperity and false blessings and you will see your stamina, your courage, and even your faith challenged like you have not experienced anywhere else.

Revival is coming, but it will not come without a fight. This will be a fight, not of physical challenges, but of the ethereal issues of spiritual deception – a much more difficult and insidious struggle than we face in the flesh. This is not for the faint-hearted. Only those who have the wisdom and spiritual discernment that comes from the fear of God need apply. All others would fall into the delusion of Satan's hypnotic sway.

And that is what has happened to so many in the Church who, at one time launched into the Gospel with all fire and zeal, only to become sophisticated and succumb to the Sirens of Prosperity and a Worldly Gospel.

Cast Your Bread Upon the Waters

While I have been here in Nigeria, I have felt like I was walking under some kind of spiritual oppression and couldn't seem to get a grip on what to report back to the folks back home. It is like walking through a heavy, dark fog.

The first two weeks here have been good. My messages were breaking ground with a lot of pastors because they remember that this very same message that I am preaching was alive in the churches here 40 years ago when the old powerhouses were here preaching and revival was burning. As one pastor put it, they used to be so desperate to win souls that they would go out into the streets to take the Gospel to the lost, but now they have retreated back into their churches, waiting for the sinners to come to them instead. Something died in the Church when that happened, and they want it back.

My core message is that the Gospel is not about you but is about others, and this resonates loudly with many of these pastors. They get it. But there are some who do not. The prevalent message of blessings, prosperity, and a more abundant life in Jesus always has more appeal than a message of blood, sacrifice, and death.

Most of the people out in the congregations get it also, but sometimes it is only for the moment. Put one of these prosperity preachers up right after me that will proclaim showers of blessings and that this is your day of victory and deliverance, and the people jump to their feet cheering, forgetting everything that I just told them.

Like any good con artist, these charlatans know exactly which buttons to push to get people on their feet. I watched aghast after one of my messages as the bishop was dismissing the crowd and gave one more prosperity call to give him money – the obvious promise being that if you want God to bless you, you have to bless the bishop. He stood there with his hand out taking money like a man selling raffle tickets. At least with raffle tickets, you stand a chance of winning something.

After so many years of being fed this American version of the Prosperity Gospel, it is going to take patience to turn this ship around. Many have itching ears and are more willing to heap to themselves teachers that will tell them what their ears itch to hear than to offer their lives as a holy sacrifice.

But not everybody. Many have come back to me to tell me that the message has transformed their outlook and that they will take the message and carry the torch to others. God will raise up those whom He will use to change the world. There may not be many. Jesus only had eleven men to entrust the entire world to and look what they did.

All we can do is cast our bread upon the waters and let God do what only He can do.

Leaving Abuja

My time here in the capital of Nigeria is half over. Tomorrow is Sunday and I will do two services in the morning and one last service in the evening at another church. Then we head for the Delta State in the south where I expect it will be a much different experience.

The first three days took place at a conference for pastors and leaders to launch a new networking organization. They aim to bring together churches and resources for a revival in Nigeria.

It was okay, I guess. I spoke to them a little about the core of my message, what my vision was, and what it would take to bring it to pass. I was just trying to be nice. These were, after all, a large group of big-shot pastors and bishops with huge ministries. Judging by their clothes, they were also pretty well-heeled. I'm just a nobody from nowhere, but I wasn't so much intimidated as I was just trying to get along with everyone.

Oh, was that a mistake!

When I opened the door to my hotel room, I could feel the Lord sitting in the corner waiting for me. He was not pleased.

"I didn't send you here to make friends with these people. I sent you here to tell them the truth!"

In no uncertain terms, I was released to bring them a much harder message of repentance than I had brought. Released. That is not the correct word. More like He ripped my head off for being too soft to make a difference.

Needless to say, I was pretty severe the next day. After laying into them for almost an hour, there was dead silence. I thought they were ready to run me out of there, but they actually welcomed it. One of the biggest pastors there asked if I would please bring this same message to his church on Sunday. That next Sunday was Easter. He handed me his church on Easter. That's a pretty good sign.

After that, we moved on to a smattering of different churches where my biggest challenge was to encapsulate as much of the message into a single service as I could. There was only one church that I was able to preach at for three services. Not surprisingly, the message would pour out with a life of its own and would touch the hearts of the whole congregation.

For pastors who are trained to "prepare" their message, it is a bit surprising to see this happen two or three times a day every day without any preparation or planning - just stand up behind the pulpit and let it rip. But what is amazing is the anointing that saturates the message. As usual, I can't feel anything, but they can. Sometimes I wonder and hope that it isn't just my passion or zeal that they feel, but that it really is the Spirit of God. They assure me that it is. One thing is for sure, <u>something</u> is breaking their hearts and bringing them to their knees.

I can't say that the services have had the dramatic results that we have seen in other countries, but

Nigerians are very different from others. I will say, however, that they have been dramatically challenged. Outlooks have been turned, hearts have been opened, and fires have been ignited. One church told me that they will not fail God in this call to revival. They will not fail! Wow. That's good enough for me. I don't need anything more supernatural than that.

The last two nights have been at a fairly well-established church. Last night they had what they call a vigil. It starts at 10 pm and lasts until 4 am. The prayer times are interspersed with mini messages and singing, so the time flies by. I delivered my soul for an hour and after I was done, the pastor requested a prayer line to form so I could "impart an anointing" into each person's life.

For the next hour or so, I prayed over one person after another. You can feel the anointing flow like a river of oil. It's almost like you're in a different medium, just floating along as the Spirit of God flows through you into their lives.

When I would look down the line, it seemed to keep getting longer, as if they were multiplying like rabbits down there. The line never ended ... and then all of a sudden, it was done. Something transforming had just taken place in the lives of these people and in the soul of this church. I believe they will never be the same.

They were touched by the Hand of God.

Balaam in Nigeria

I have left Abuja and Benin and am now in the Delta State with a bishop who is in charge of a large network of churches throughout Nigeria. The people I am with now are so excited that they have given me a place to stay and have provided for anything I need. They won't even let me pay for my own laundry soap. What a welcome change! The place is nice, quiet, and secluded. Perfect for me.

Nevertheless, I am constantly worn out and drained of energy. There is something in the air that is oppressive and heavy. My theory is that we are trudging through spiritual warfare against the prince of the air. Yeah, I'll bet a lot of folks in America would dismiss all the talk about witchcraft as superstitious, but if you spend enough time over here, you will change your mind. Every day it feels like you're moving in a spiritual cloud.

Today I could barely move. It was like I was drugged or something and I just couldn't snap out of it. Then the sharp pains started coming in my guts as I was getting up to the pulpit to preach. I don't know what the devil was afraid of, because I was so fuzzy-headed that I had no clue as to what I was going to preach about, but oh boy, was I in pain! I seriously started wondering if I was going to have to pack it in and head for the hospital. I can't die cause I'm not finished, but the devil can make it so that I <u>feel</u> like I'm dying.

And then, as soon as I started preaching through the pain, whoosh! It was gone. Yeah, just like that. That's always the case with this kind of stuff. As soon as the anointing comes down, the darkness flees. I can always tell that it is going to be a blockbuster message when I get horribly sick just before I get up to the pulpit. Today was even more pronounced. I did two services and headed back to the house to collapse on the bed. Honestly, I really think there is a concerted effort to resist me in the spiritual realm. I can't prove it, and I know how crazy it sounds, but that's the only thing that makes sense.

But that also means that we are striking a nerve. If my theory is correct, Nigeria is the last spiritual fortress to conquer before revival can sweep across Africa. Satan knows it, and in order for him to delay the coming of Jesus and his own destruction, he has to stop the revival here.

He's not going to rely upon the Muslims or Boko Haram or even the sinners to cause us trouble – he will use the Church. His biggest weapon is to lull the spiritually naïve into a lullaby of blessings, peace, love and focus their attention on themselves. This is how Satan used Balaam to teach the people of God to sin. And it almost worked. He's trying it again here in Nigeria.

This is what I am fighting against, and it is a desperate battle for the soul of Africa and by extension, the rest of the world. If revival cannot break out here where people are so desperately hungry for God, how could it ever happen in America where we are so asleep that we are not able to admit that there's anything wrong with us?

Please hold Nigeria up in your prayers. I believe there is more at stake here than just a simple missionary trip. This may be the beginning volleys before the final battle between God and Satan.

Souls of the Needy

I woke up at 5:30 this morning to hands clapping and voices singing praises to God.

It was still dark and there was nothing else stirring outside. I had just been waking up and could feel the early morning stirrings around me, and then all of a sudden, came these voices from the living room. First one, then another, and soon they were joined by everyone else in the house. What a wonderful way to open up the morning!

My host and I have been staying in a home on the outskirts of Agbor, Nigeria, and last night we were joined by some of the pastors in his network along with their daughters to stay overnight and help with the house. They were all there in the living room singing when I stumbled in.

After a song or two, one of the pastors read some scriptures and we started praying. We prayed short, directed prayers of thanksgiving for the different things that God has done for us. Then we prayed concentrated prayers against all the different ways that Satan would try to attack us this day. Africans are intimately aware of the reality of the powers of darkness and what they are capable of. Finally, we rounded it up with prayers for God to bestow power and blessings upon our ministries today and send revival. Did we miss anything?

Do they do this every day? I think so. It seemed as natural to them at 5:30 in the morning as an everyday routine. Whether or not they will continue in prayer throughout the day is another thing, but they sure started it off right.

The African heart is more open and bare to God than ours in the West, and their souls are needier. God looms much larger in their lives and fills the horizon of their vision, whereas, with us, God has to compete for our attention with all the distractions that we have filled our lives with. Small wonder He is so attentive to their prayers. Maybe that's why there are so many miracles here.

Last night we had another healing line after services. Close to thirty people came up to be prayed over. They did not come up to have the white man sprinkle fairy dust and share his blessing upon them; they came up to have God touch them and heal them. And He did. With only a few exceptions, I could feel the anointing flow through them as God healed one after another. I would ask them to make sure, "Are you healed?" "Yes! The pain is gone!", as they would turn and raise their hands in thanks to God.

Yeah. It just doesn't get much better than this. And I had a seat right up front to experience it firsthand.

In writing about the Azusa Street Revival, Rick Joiner commented, "When it was learned that the greatest demonstrations of the Spirit's power usually came in the darkest, neediest places, many were compelled to go on mission trips just to witness the power of God." Amen. Want to see the fire? Want to feel the Anointing? Want to witness the power? Want to see God move? Come to Africa!

"For he shall deliver the needy when he crieth; the poor also, and him that hath no helper. He shall spare the poor and needy, and shall save the souls of the needy." (Psalms 72:12-13)

The Yard

I share the yard with some other creatures as if I am a guest passing through who will be gone tomorrow while they remain. There is the tiny black and white bird with a long tail who has claimed a domain over the two skinny saplings out front. The trees are no bigger than 15 feet tall and only boast of some leaves at the very top like a green leafy cap resting upon their skinny heads, but those trees are his trees however small and emaciated they may appear to us.

His two split tail feathers are longer than the rest of his body and dangle and whip behind him like the tail of a kite. Whenever another bird comes to rest upon one of the branches of his trees, he immediately jumps into the air, fluttering and dancing in the air before them, whipping his tail back and forth, and chasing them from branch to branch until the intruder flies off for a more peaceful resting place.

At first, I thought this was a mating dance that he, as the more colorful and plumed of the species performed in desperation for his prospective lady who would sit in her drably-colored dress of dull brown feathers and decide whether or not he was good enough for her. But in seeing how he would aggressively pursue these little brown birds until they left, I now realized that this was not a love dance, but a territorial one. And maybe he wasn't a he; maybe he was a she who was guarding her future nest. I've known some women like that.

While the trees belonged to the little long-tailed bird, the ground belonged to a red and black lizard who I dubbed Big Red. He is a strangely colored animal – head a reddish-orange, body a dark purplish-black, his rump a stark white, and his tail following the same sequence of red, black, and white down to the tip. He looks like one of those rubber toys you get for your little boys to play with – he doesn't look real. But he is most definitely in charge of the yard.

A worn-out wall of eroded blocks surrounds the property here. The blocks that are used in Africa are sandy and not as durable as we are accustomed to, so rain has a deteriorating effect on them making them look as if they are part of some ancient ruins. It is on this terrain that this king holds his court. No one is allowed here without his permission (unless, of course, you are bigger than him). Nigeria is teeming with lizards. He would chase other lizards, and if he did not think that they were sufficiently intimidated, he would grab hold of them with his mouth and shake them until they ran away. Tough little scooter.

I share this yard with them and a few others as a passing visitor. Nigeria is not my home, nor would I want it to be. This is a hard place.

But for many like Big Red and his feisty long-tailed neighbor, however, it is home, and it is worth fighting for.

Back into the Battle

And Jesus went into the temple of God, and cast out all them that sold and bought in the temple, and overthrew the tables of the moneychangers, and the seats of them that sold doves,

And said unto them, It is written, My house shall be called the house of prayer; but ye have made it a den of thieves.

And the blind and the lame came to him in the temple; and he healed them.

(Matthew 21:12-14)

Off to Nigeria Again

I'm sitting in the airport surrounded by Nigerians on their way home. This will make the fifth or sixth trip to Nigeria for me, but unlike the crowd of Africans around me that returning to familiar homes, I feel like an invader coming into a foreign land. Nigeria has never been comfortable for me.

There are two reasons: one is cultural; the other is prophetic.

I have found Nigeria to be a hard place. This is a strong people in a difficult country. Whether that is because of the over-population, the incredible amount of corruption that comes as a result of huge amounts of oil money, or something in their blood, Nigerians are a strong people in the midst of a social conflict in a hard land.

The other reason may be considered debatable depending on what your view of the end times is. I believe that Nigeria is key to the rest of the sub-Saharan continent. In order for revival to fully sweep across Africa, Nigeria must fall to the dominion of Jesus Christ. There is just something about these people that strike me as a cornerstone for Africa. I believe that Satan knows that also, and for that very reason, he has entrenched himself deeply into the Nigerian Church.

It's not the Muslims that are the biggest threat, or even the criminal element. Even the wickedness in the political leadership is being driven by this darkness. It is the wickedness that is found in the depths of the established Nigerian Church that is the fountain that contaminates their society.

On the surface, it would seem that Lagos is the most religious city in the world, but underlying that are deep pools of wickedness. No matter where you go, you will see posters and signs declaring the next Night of Miracles at one meeting or the Showers of Blessings at another. Religious names are everywhere as if it is a lucky charm for retail businesses to be called the Glory to God Cafe or the Heavenly Blessings gas station.

And yet, Lagos remains one of the most corrupt cities in the world. Why is that? Reinhardt Bonke can have his million-person crusades here, but on the next day, nothing has changed. There is something endemic that Satan has buried deep in the Nigerian culture that resists true holiness in God. The signs are there, the talk is there, even the outward show is there, but something is missing.

I am here to preach revival and to plant a seed of resistance to the debilitating messages of prosperity and the weakening influence of their false prophets. I am not the usual evangelist with the usual message of peace and love and grace. I have a truly Biblical prophetic message: repentance, righteousness, and the fear of God. Real peace and love and mercy grow out of righteousness into true charity and a deep, driving burden to win the lost. There is a huge difference between these two messages.

And I think that is what is missing here – true

holiness and unselfish charity. It is the message I have brought across Africa for 15 years and has worked everywhere I have preached it. I pray God it will work here.

The world is waiting for this last, great revival to start, and this is one of the last obstacles to be removed.

Miracles, Money, and Faith

The Bishop's wife got healed last night, but the blind lady did not. I don't know why.

Yesterday was the beginning of a 3-day session in Ashaka, Nigeria. My main objective is to somehow inspire the people here to not just hear and believe the message but to be driven to the point that they will go out into the streets to bring in the lost and start the process for a true revival. Healing the Bishop's wife wasn't part of it.

It was a great service, but as I was heading out the door after the service, this skinny, little old lady stopped me and asked me to pray over her. I wasn't sure what was wrong with her or who she was, but she looked pretty sick. We prayed and her face lit up as the Spirit came down and touched her. She was healed! I didn't know what to do at that point other than get in the car and collapse in the seat for the ride back to the hotel.

Well, it turns out she was the Bishop's wife, and she was sick with Malaria and some other nasty diseases. Not only did she get instantly healed, but she went and told everybody. As you can guess, they all wanted to have a healing line after the message.

Now, when I do healing lines, I don't pray for the whole group at one time; that just does not work for me. I have to do it one at a time. I want to know exactly what is wrong with them and that's what we pray for. Then I ask them if they are healed, and if they are not, we pray again. If they still are not healed, then we pray a third time. If they are not healed after three times, then there is something else at work here and I have to give it into the hands of God.

Some got healed; some did not. There was a blind lady that I just could not lift the cover that lay over her faith. It was as if she was afraid to believe. Sometimes, you will pray over someone and you can just feel that resistance hampering the prayer of faith. Getting past that barrier can sometimes be nigh unto impossible, at least as far as I have experienced. That barrier has to be broken to release their faith to believe that God sees you, He hears you, He cares about you, and yes, He will heal you. That is the key to releasing their faith to believe and be healed. Sometimes that is so hard that you just can't pray through it.

I prayed twice over her and it just did not happen. But next to her was someone with a sickness who did get healed. Several others also came up with pains, headaches, stomach things, and a couple of weird things that I have no idea what I was laying my hands on — they all got healed except the blind lady.

I have no idea why that happens like that. I have experienced this hundreds of times and still have no idea. It just does. Period. Was it my faith, their faith, sin, doubt, or just plain "that's the way it is"? I'm going to go with the last one. Somebody who has never healed anyone in their life will probably write a book and tell us all about how it is supposed to be done, but in the meantime, with as many times as I have done this, I know less than I did when I started.

I believe, however, that healing miracles are not the prime focus of ministry, but are God's seal of approval. The focus of our ministry should be to save the lost. What good would it be to have someone healed and wind up in Hell? The Lord once told me that miracles take away from the message. Once the stampede starts for the miracles, they will no longer be listening to the message. I have found that to be true, which is why I try to wait for the end before we have healing lines. But tonight, everybody wanted what the Bishop's wife got last night.

My great fear is that after all that is preached, prayed, and repented, I would be little more than a temporary entertainment, and the fire that I had kindled would be allowed to slowly die out. I want them to do more than just cheer and shout; I want them to do. I would love to see everybody get healed, but, more than that, I want to see them start a fire of revival so that everybody would get saved.

I have had great successes in East Africa, Uganda, Burundi, Rwanda, and the Congo, but Nigeria is a tough venue. We are being told everywhere we go that this message is what Nigeria needs and pastors are excited to get the book and spread the message further. But we are up against an incredibly strong prosperity, wealth, and cheap grace movement in the Nigerian Church that is diametrically opposed to the doctrine of repentance, holiness, and the fear of God. It will be a long and hard battle to crack the wall of this corrupt established Church, but these are strong men and women, so when this message of revival does get a foothold, I believe it will explode.

The odds do not favor us. They are the same odds that were against the children of Israel in Egypt, David with King Saul, John the Baptist with King Herod, and Jesus with the Sanhedrin. Paul faced the challenge of converting the entire known world all the while being attacked by the Circumcision heretics, but it was said that he and Silas had turned the world upside down (Acts 17:6).

We are facing the same odds. May the best man win.

From the Pool of Siloam

Well, today the blind man got healed. Along with about 100 others. No, really. It was somewhere around that many. Including the blind man who came up to me after services to tell me that he had received his sight. All he said was three words, "I can see", but that encapsulated the entire Gospel for me and the reason why we are here.

It didn't start with that many. The pastor called for anyone who needed healing to come up and about 25 or so came. But, oh boy, once people saw that everybody was getting healed, the crowd started growing. And kept growing. They were multiplying like rabbits out there. It took almost another two hours to finally get through the line.

Why is it that the healing miracles always seem to take center stage when telling these stories? I guess hearing about something supernatural that is so far outside our normal scope of life is exciting. It's certainly exciting to be a part of, and it's exciting to tell. And, it can be pretty exciting if you're the one getting healed. But the miracles are not the important part of the service. The message is what is important. The central point to this whole thing is to see souls won.

And we did win souls at this service. Besides the hundred or so that got healed, fifty souls got saved. (I didn't count them; the pastor's wife did.) For the hundred souls that got healed, life has become better, immeasurably so for some of them. For the fifty who got saved, however, their entire lives have just changed, and they will never be the same. And yet, it is the healing miracles that get the headlines.

For me, I can only say that it is exciting to see the hand of God work right in front of your eyes. Maybe because healings are more visible, they seem to capture our attention more. But I don't always feel the anointing pass through me when they get healed. Sometimes I do. It can be like electricity shooting through you, and sometimes there is a sensation of oil flowing through you, but most of the time it is just pure faith.

Sometimes I sense a deeper presence of faith when I pray than at other times, and I have to believe that is the Spirit of God that I am sensing, but the truth is, most of the time I don't feel anything. The real blessing, however, is when they tell you that the disease/pain/ailment is gone. It's gone. It was there and now it is gone! That's what wows me every time.

I love preaching revival messages and watching churches catch the fire. It's like flipping a switch of understanding and turning on the furnace. To hear that a church that I just preached to has been set on fire has started putting the principles I've told them to work, and has multiplied the size of the congregation several times over is a tremendous gratification for me. It is the main purpose I have come. It is what we have sacrificed so much for. There's nothing better than to hear the grand vision we have had is being fulfilled and birthed in church after church.

But then, there's that blind man that got healed.

Why does that capture the headline for me? I guess for me it is because it is the embodiment of the entire mission of revival distilled down to a deeply personal level right before my eyes. This morning he was blind, in darkness, and without hope, but now he can see and everything has changed.

"...one thing I know, that, whereas I was blind, now I see." (John 9:25)

With Such People

Wow, what a service. This is the kind of thing that makes it all worthwhile.

We are in Abbi, Nigeria, a small town buried deep in the delta country around the Niger River. Driving through the lush countryside to get here, you pass scenes of deep poverty everywhere. There is little to sustain an economy here other than subsistence farming, and it is reflected in the shambles of wooden shacks and unfinished buildings.

You feel rather than see the poverty, but there is also a feeling that life here is not that bad. The kids are running around having fun, adults are working at peeling cassava or other agrarian tasks to provide dinner. There isn't a feeling of stress or anxiety at not having all the luxuries of modern society. Maybe our idea of what to strive for in life is a bit inflated. Maybe they have something better, small though it may be.

Heading into services, I am pressed with what message to present these people. This is not a big, powerful church with a thousand members. This is the same kind of small, personal congregation that I am used to ministering to. They are just little people, but I have to somehow convince these people that they can change the world.

Sometimes I have to look up and double-check with Him, "Are You sure this is where I am supposed to be?"

The answer is always, "Yes, this is how I show my glory." He uses small things. Broken things. Things that others discard for being too weak, too small, too poor, too useless, because He will not share His glory with man.

I fit right in there with them. Who am I, really? I'm a nobody. I have no credentials, degrees, church, or even a small organization. I have no money of my own to speak of, and back in America, no one knows who I am, and neither do they care.

But here, I fit in like a hand in a glove. They know who I am. And they have a long list of titles for me: Doctor, prophet, bishop, pastor, apostle, father, and now just recently, Mentor. But it's not me they honor. I am a nobody who carries the anointing and presence of God to them, and that's what they are hungry for.

I am very much aware of the fact that I can't bring revival - only God can - but God will use anyone willing to humble themselves, throw away the pride and positions of ecclesiastical authority, and just show up crucified, broken, and poor. Since I possess so little anyway, that is not hard for me. My job is to show up; God does the rest.

Last night, the entire congregation was on its knees before God in sincere repentance for not winning souls. Everybody. Including the ushers, including the pastor, everyone. Try that back in America. Have we become so enamored with ourselves and our prosperity that we can no longer humble ourselves to that degree, but instead have become the Church of Laodicea? Jonah said, *"They that observe lying vanities, forsake their own mercy."* (Jonah

2:8)

I may be a nobody ministering to small, seemingly inconsequential churches in a poor land beleaguered by satanic forces, fake prosperity preachers, and false prophets, but it is with such people that God uses to build His kingdom.

"But God hath chosen the foolish things of the world to confound the wise; and God hath chosen the weak things of the world to confound the things which are mighty"
(1 Corinthians 1:27)

Signs of Revival

I am on the way home. It has been three weeks of intense spiritual warfare, and while I may not have won every battle, we have come through in victory. Only eternity will reveal what has happened during this 3-week campaign.

This trip has been one of the hardest that I have been on in years. The spiritual "headfire" that I went through was like being in the midst of a hurricane blowing at full force while in the middle of a swarm of angry bees. This was not everyday stuff, but something that reached a level of intensity reserved for a deep, serious battle. I'm not going to say I won every battle, but I did make it through. And it was not easy.

I have always believed that whenever there is a lot of resistance and spiritual fire from Satan, something big must be going on. He is not stupid. He knows when there is a strong threat to his hold and he will fight like a wildcat to stop it or at least slow it down. So the question is, what was Satan so riled up about? What happened that made him go crazy on me like that? What are the indications that we were so effective that he had to pull out all the stops to fight us like that?

A lot of souls came down to the altar and either gave their lives to Christ or repented for sin and made a rededication. Scores of people were healed, some with serious afflictions. At least three blind people received their sight. But, while these things are exciting and seem to indicate that the campaign was a great success, they are not the true signs of our effectiveness.

Just like you can tell the depth of any church or ministry by certain telltale signs (blood, fire, fear, and souls is a message I have written about before), so can you tell the effectiveness of any campaign by some signs that, on the surface, may not seem so obvious.

Counting the number of souls that came down to the altar is NOT one of those signs.

Evangelism is easily promoted with things that will draw a crowd and even bring them down to the altar. I have watched evangelists call out to the crowd that everyone that comes down will get a free book on how to live for Christ. Guess what everybody did – they went down to get something for free. And the evangelist can now count the books and tell his supporters back home how many thousands of souls have been saved.

Or an internationally known evangelist can hand out $60,000 in cash to the local pastors to bring their people to the meeting and he will take credit for all the people that attended and boast of his great effectiveness to the folks back home, but the day after the evangelist leaves, the corruption is still the same. Nothing really changed. It sounded good, but its long-term effectiveness was only a ripple.

Oh yes, I know soul-winning is the primary goal of the Church. It's what we do, what we strive for, and that burden for souls is the secret to revival, but just having a large soul count is not an indication of the long-term effectiveness of any campaign. What counts is how much the churches that were part of the campaign have changed over time. A month later, have those churches gone back to their same old ways, or have they been revolutionized, turned inside out, and set on fire? Let's take another soul count after a month or so and see if the seed has not only been planted in good ground but has germinated and is beginning to push out of the fallow ground that has been broken up and watered with tears of repentance and prayer for souls.

The sign of the campaign's effectiveness is not the number that came down to the altar during your campaign, but the number of souls that continue to get saved and the number of churches that were planted as a result.

Prayer is the other sign. Serious, passionate prayer is essential to any move of God and is the true sign that the campaign for that church has been effective. Some places face difficult persecution and hardships that make any growth slow. Their challenges, like a huge boulder in the path, must be moved slowly with patience and a persevering faith that will not be discouraged because of a lack of fanfare and showmanship. But what you will find in those places, if the seed has been planted well, is a greater depth and dimension of prayer.

Nothing moves without prayer. No battles can be won that are not first won in the prayer room. Every move of God must first be birthed in that labor room of prayer. No revival happens without it because prayer moves God. Some campaigns grow faster than others.

Some have initial successes that fizzle out, while others continue to grow over time, but in order for a move of God to be established, the atmosphere of prayer must be established and be foundational to any campaign. When you do not see a church saturated in prayer, no matter how exciting their initial success is, it will not prosper.

If you want to see how any church is doing, check their Wednesday night prayer meeting. That is the thermostat that determines the measure of fire in any church. We can all make a lot of noise about all the great things that have happened, but the real fire is only lit by the torch that burns in the prayer room.

So how did we do in Nigeria these past three weeks? I'll tell you in a month or so when we see if the seed has germinated in good ground, if the repentance was true and heartfelt, and if the door to the altar of prayer has been opened in their lives to light the torch of revival.

I am the vine, ye are the branches: He that abideth in me, and I in him, the same bringeth forth much fruit: for without me ye can do nothing. (John 15:5)

A Last Campaign

Therefore, also now, saith the LORD, turn ye even to me with all your heart, and with fasting, and with weeping, and with mourning: And rend your heart, and not your garments, and turn unto the LORD your God: for he is gracious and merciful, slow to anger, and of great kindness, and repenteth him of the evil.

Who knoweth if he will return and repent, and leave a blessing behind him; even a meat offering and a drink offering unto the LORD your God?

Blow the trumpet in Zion, sanctify a fast, call a solemn assembly: Gather the people, sanctify the congregation, assemble the elders, gather the children, and those that suck the breasts: let the bridegroom go forth of his chamber, and the bride out of her closet.

Let the priests, the ministers of the LORD, weep between the porch and the altar, and let them say, Spare thy people, O LORD, and give not thine heritage to reproach, that the heathen should rule over them: wherefore should they say among the people, Where is their God?

Then will the LORD be jealous for his land and pity his people.

(Joel 2:12-18)

Letting Go of the Seed

"And he said, So is the kingdom of God, as if a man should cast seed into the ground; And should sleep, and rise night and day, and the seed should spring and grow up, he knoweth not how.

For the earth bringeth forth fruit of herself; first the blade, then the ear, after that the full corn in the ear. But when the fruit is brought forth, immediately he putteth in the sickle, because the harvest is come." (Mark 4:26-29)

I am sitting in the airport waiting for my flight that will take me back into Africa, the Dark Continent. This is the beginning of this year's retinue of revival campaigns. There will be a total of six of them from Nigeria to Kenya. But I hope that this will be the last sweep before I turn the commission over to the next generation.

Back in 2004, when I first came here, the Lord gave me a vision of a harvest field of wheat that was so dry that it had turned a brittle white. I watched as I stepped into the field, struck a match, and dropped it into the dry, brittle grass. The field exploded on fire and spread across Africa from Kenya to Nigeria.

That was 15 years ago. I have seen lots of fires break out in several countries, I have listened to many pastors and leaders who have been set on fire themselves, and have heard of thousands of souls that have been saved and lit up, but the Great African Revival, the explosive blaze that I saw has yet to come. The Lord didn't promise me that I would see it - He just told me to strike the matches that would light it.

It is time to step back and let the seeds that have been sown across the landscape settle into the soil, die and germinate, and then grow up into the harvest. I have sown; someone else will reap.

There is a lesson here that I have learned. Actually, several lessons. One is to learn to let go of the vision and allow God to bring it forth. No matter how vital that vision is to your self-identify as a Christian, nevertheless, it is God's vision to fulfill. There is an element of faith that must be exercised to allow that to happen. You have to trust God that He will finish the vision. It's okay. You can let go.

The other lesson, at least for me, is that none of us stands alone. No matter which part of the process we are part of, we all share in the victory, but God gets all the glory. The guy preaching to 65,000 people is part of the same body as the little woman who gave two mites. Understanding the quicksand of that desire for recognition and self-glory is paramount to have any effectiveness in the battle to win souls. One of the 6 Principles of Revival is that the Gospel is not about you; it is about others. It doesn't matter which part you played. It just matters that you were part of it.

I wonder if Paul felt this way on his last journey. He had imparted his very soul to these Gentile churches only to see the enemy try to wrench them away with every kind of demonic tactic. He saw those close to him leave him. At one point only Luke was with him. Did he wonder if the seeds he planted would take growth and spread? There was no guarantee that anything would happen other than the commission from God to spread the message amongst the Gentiles. Did he know? Did he wonder?

I have to believe that whether or not Paul had a firm grip on what the future would bring, he set his face toward the goal and claimed victory knowing that regardless of his best efforts, God was and always is in control.

"I have fought a good fight, I have finished my course, I have kept the faith:" (2nd Timothy 4:7)

First Day Skirmishes

Things started going bad when the local Nigerian airline that was to take me to the city where I will be ministering just decided to cancel all flights that day. Gee, did you forget to tell me this vital piece of information when I purchased the tickets? I should've known then that the fun was about to begin.

So I had to fly to an alternate city that was hours away from where I was to end up. That's okay. I got to see the countryside. I'm just hoping that they don't decide that I have to return through that same city instead of my original route. This is Africa. Things don't always make sense.

Then, when I came out of the terminal, no one was there to pick me up. I figured that with the distance they had to travel to come to get me, I should not be surprised.   And if not, it would just add to the adventure!

I went back into the terminal to buy a SIM card for my phone and a WiFi hotspot so I could stay in touch with everyone back home. 17,500 Naira later, which is around $55.00, I thought I was pretty slick. I not only now had full cell phone coverage but also full internet access wherever I went.

I should've known.

The telephone network I had did not have any reception at the hotel that I am staying at. And guess what? That also means the WiFi doesn't either.

And do they have WiFi at the hotel?

"Oh yes, we have WiFi."

"Does it work?"

"Oh yes, it works."

"Does it work right now?"

"Well ..."

In the meantime, Cindy hasn't heard from me since two continents ago. Is he alive? Dead? Crashed? Where is he?

But hey, the services were great! Today, I was to speak at a national convention for a large network of Nigerian churches. And they were all there from the 90-year-old Archbishop to the pastors, singers, and choir. It was a 6-hour long meeting that included everything, including an hour-long message of repentance from me. It was an opportunity for me to insert a different message into their lives — something they are not used to hearing, especially from a preacher from America.

In the end, when I was wrapping up the message, I felt the Lord lead me into an Altar Call for these pastors. I could feel the Lord push me hard, so I pushed them hard. I didn't much care if they were pastors, bishops, prophets, or what they were. I have been down too many miles on too many roads to be impressed with titles. If God was pushing me, then I was pushing them.

And here they came. A dribble at first, but as the fire caught, they came. Not just repentance for sin, but for a fresh anointing, a new fire, a bigger vision. They want a gospel that is not in name only, but in the Spirit and power of Elijah. They believed me when I proclaimed that the greatest revival is coming and will start here in Africa. They believed me when I told them that God doesn't use the big and powerful; He uses the "foolish things of the world to confound the wise", the little people, the weak, and the people just like them to bring about the great works of God.

They believed me, and they believed God. They grabbed hold of the substance of things hoped for and came to the altar.

Getting Out of the Way

"In those days came John the Baptist, preaching in the wilderness of Judaea, And saying, Repent ye: for the kingdom of heaven is at hand.

For this is he that was spoken of by the prophet Esaias, saying, The voice of one crying in the wilderness, Prepare ye the way of the Lord, make his paths straight."(Matthew 3:1-3)

I have finished the 2nd day of conferences. We had one in the morning and one in the evening, and wow, were they on fire!

I have a long list of messages for the seminars that I hold. Normally, I might switch around the messages or meld them together as the Spirit leads. They might not follow the chapters in the book, but they get the message out. I never know what message I am going to preach until I am sitting in the church praying for God to tell me what to do. He always does, even though I am always afraid that I will fall flat. But I never do.

But it has been different on this trip. Maybe because I've been here before and these people know who I am, or maybe the times are changing, but the Lord just inserted two completely brand new messages to sew into the fabric of the campaign. One has to do with tithing your first fruits and how that affects the opening for revival. The other has to do with loving the brethren so much that you are willing to lay down your life for them and how that affects not only our love for lost souls, but for God Himself. Without a genuine love for your brothers, the lost, and for God, you won't see a genuine revival.

The things that were more exciting than the messages, however, were the services themselves. I could tell they were going to be good because just before each service, I'd get that same old fear that I didn't know what to preach and that I was going to fail. But that also came with a little puff of the Spirit that reassured me to not worry because He's got this. I remember one time in Nigeria, the Lord actually spoke to me, "Do you trust Me?", and my answer was, "Yes, Lord. You lead, and I'll follow."

I told them today that my job is to first show up and then get out of the way. I showed up all three days and I will show up the rest of the week. I also got out of the way, and when I did, He took over the message.

I can't explain to you what it's like to have God take over the message. Today's ministers do not allow for that because they've been trained to prepare their messages long before they come to the pulpit. I was taught to prepare yourself in the Spirit, surrender your control, open your mouth, and He will fill it. It's like He is riding on top of you, leaning you into every direction that He wants you to go in. All you have to do is let go and hang on for the ride.

When the Spirit of God is giving the message, it is always filled with fire. And that's what these messages have been like. And that's coming from the pastors that are experiencing these services.

When I was coming to Nigeria last week, I was dealing with the question of how to create inspiration and desire in the hearts of people for revival, for serving the Lord, and for going out to win souls. Once again, I got my answer - show up, and get out of the way! This is not your battle, they are not your people, and it is not your message - it all belongs to God. You just have to prepare the way before Him.

That's what John the Baptist did, and that's what we are called to do today.

First Couple Days of Excitement

Services have been electrifying here. We've been having one service in the morning and another in the evening, which, considering the intensity that I preach with, makes this very exhausting. I end each service soaked with sweat and limp as a wet dishrag. And yet, I have been at my best and in my prime, which is saying something because it has been months since I have been in the saddle.

Each message has had a brand new element added to it. One such message added how tithing your first fruits was tied to revival. Giving your firsts, not only money, but time, heart, and soul, to the cause of winning the lost releases you by breaking that spirit of selfishness and greed. The 2nd Principle of Revival is that the Gospel is not about you; it is about others, and tithing breaks that hold that "self" has on you. You cannot serve God and Mammon. If you are committed to revival, then for Heaven's sake, invest in it! *"Where your treasure is..."*

At another service, I read out of James 1:22 about being doers of the Word and not hearers only, deceiving your selves. The deception is that you can languish in your apostasy without ever doing anything but sitting in that same pew for years, and still believe that you will go to Heaven. Maybe you will, but I'm not laying odds on it. But one thing's for certain - you will not see revival burst out over you.

My business cards have my ministry information on one side and a 6-point Plan of Salvation on the back. This morning, I handed every person two of my cards - one to keep (otherwise they'd never give the other one away) and one to pass out to a complete stranger. The idea was to kick-start the idea of witnessing. Guess what? They did it! I thought I was going to catch them in this, but instead, they were on their feet excited because they had actually done it - they had overcome their fears and handed a Gospel tract to a total stranger. Revival is on the way.

Something else happened yesterday morning that I felt pretty good about. I could feel that there was someone that needed prayer, whether for sin or some demonic stranglehold, and that they should come up at some point in time. This is one of those things that many preachers understand. You just get this chilling feeling and you know there is somebody out there who has to come to the altar today. At the end of the service, a small woman pastor came up who was in bondage to a spirit of fear. I laid hands on her and it was like a bolt of lightning shot through me. Bam! Down she went, and that spirit of fear was broken. She was so happy she was jumping up and down, grinning from ear to ear. And she was like that the next day also!

Today, however, I was able to do something really cool. I wanted to demonstrate the power of healing that is given to all of us to exercise. Mark 16 says so. So I asked if anyone had a headache, and some lady stood up. I laid hands on her and, bingo! she was healed. Just like always. I have yet to meet a headache that I couldn't heal. But then, I asked for another person with a headache and another lady stood up. This time I took a guy at random out of the congregation and made <u>him</u> pray over her. Yup, you guessed it - she was healed. Can you imagine the excitement that went through the room? Wow. Nobody had ever done that with them. Just the idea that <u>they</u> could do this - not somebody else – they could!

The idea of healing is more than God's mercy to us in our infirmities. It is a sign or a seal of approval that God is truly with us. And if He can heal, He can deliver. And if He can deliver, He can save us. I sincerely believe that once you start healing people out there, they will start coming. But the people of God have to believe that God has really given us this promise and that if we will just exercise our faith, what wonders we will see.

I'm pretty jazzed (did you notice?), and I can see that these people are too. Good things, — <u>big</u> things— are bound to come out of these meetings. And that's why it doesn't matter what it costs, how hard it is, or what I have to sacrifice to be here, I have got to take this message of revival to as many places as I can. Before my knees buckle, my back gives in, and my voice goes hoarse, Lord, let me see this fire explode around the world.

"Now also when I am old and gray-headed, O God, forsake me not; until I have showed thy strength unto this generation, and thy power to everyone that is to come." (Psalms 71:18)

Last Day of the Campaign in Nigeria

"And Saul was consenting unto his death. And at that time there was a great persecution against the church which was at Jerusalem; and they were all scattered abroad throughout the regions of Judaea and Samaria, except the apostles." Acts 8:1

I threatened them today.

Well, actually, the Lord threatened them. Acts 8:1-4 talks of the persecution that came upon the early church at Jerusalem. God had commissioned them to go into all the world and make disciples, but they were comfortable right where they were at and were not in any rush to leave. Life was good. Thousands were getting saved. Miracles were happening daily, there was joy in the streets and real love amongst the brethren. Why would anyone want to head off into the world of the Gentiles?

Because they wouldn't go forth out of Jerusalem to preach the Gospel, God used persecution to chase them out. You don't believe God would do that? Compare that to Egypt. They were there in slavery for 144 years*, but when they finally cried out to God, He sent the Deliverer. Why did it take so long for them to cry out to God? I don't know, maybe they just got used to the way things were. Maybe the slavery you know is better than taking a chance on a liberty that you don't know. But when their babies began to be murdered, they started crying out to God. And when they did, God sent Moses.

I gave them a chilling prophecy of what is coming to them if they don't get out of their lazy white plastic chairs and go make disciples. You could feel the cold seriousness in the room as they sat on the edge of their chairs staring at me. It happened to the Israelites back then; it could happen to them right now.

Yesterday was also question and answer time. Boy, they came up with some sharp questions — they always do. They kept me on my toes, but I answered everyone one of their questions, even the tough ones. I will be first to admit that I don't know everything. One of the most important lessons I ever learned was that is it okay to say you don't know. But I have one advantage in these sessions — I got God. I'm not just saying that because it makes a good sound byte. No, it is true — He gives me the answers. I might stumble around for a minute or so, but it always comes. And when it comes, it is always perfect. That's how I know it's not from me.

One of the questions was about how to tell when you are being led by the Spirit of God and when you're being led by your own spirit. They are very aware of the dangers of the false prophets that plague their churches. Just like us, they have a whole raft of well-known personalities posing as "God's Generals" to hand down meaningless prophesies of peace, prosperity, wealth, and blessings. Never about repentance or holiness. How is it that they are so much more aware of this than we are? I can only guess it is because they are more spiritually sensitive than we are in the West. So, this was a big question for them. And yes, God gave me the answer.

We're almost done, and I am tired. My voice is so hoarse that I can barely speak, but somehow, I keep punching out one more service. You know how it works - when there is no strergth, the Anointing carries you. They have seen that, and they realize what it is.

It just makes the message so much more important to them. God is talking tc them. And they are listening.

---

* Israel's Time of 3ojourning from the Promise to the Exodus was 430 years, but the time that they were in slavery would not have started until after Joseph's death which was only 144 years from the Exodus.

Meet for the Master's Use

The call to bring revival to a nation is not something that can be accomplished through any strength or wisdom that we possess in ourselves. No matter how badly you want to plunge into the fray and proclaim liberty in the land, the power to bring the presence and power of God that will ignite the Church is not something that can be flippantly learned in Seminary or produced with any theologically designed program. Only God can do that, and only when we are in complete surrender are we able to lend ourselves as crucified vessels that He can work through.

Frank Bartleman, in recounting an encounter he had with the Lord, wrote that the Lord told him after he had received the Baptism of the Holy Ghost, *"If you were only small enough, I could do anything with you."*

Ah, here's lies the crux, almost a Catch-22 if you would. How does one maintain, or better put, achieve that place of true humility so that God can use you to do His mighty works? On the one hand, we strive to get to that place of righteousness to have power in God while at the same time, we try to be in that broken, crucified walk in God so we can be yielded to His power. How does one strike that perfect balance? Sounds simple ... or is it?

David had it; Saul did not. Perhaps that was because, for Saul, it was always about Saul. When he was little in his own eyes, he was hiding amongst the stuff, but a couple of years later, he was such a big shot that he didn't think he had to wait on God's prophet. For David, on the other hand, it was never about David; it was always about God. Because of that, he was able to take on Goliath as a kid, and later as an adult with just two other guys, the entire Philistine army. (2nd Samuel 23:9)

Any man of God who has had the power of God work through him will immediately be attacked by the enemy. Whether it is miracle healings, dynamic preaching, or supernatural revelation, no sooner does one experience the touch of God's hand than that little wisp of a thought will pass through the back of your mind that, yes it was God's power, but ... ahem ... He did choose to use you!

Satan will sneak those thoughts in as lightly and subtly as he can. If you think about it hard enough, you will recognize the devil's handiwork, so he keeps as light a touch as he can ... and then another ... and then another, merging them ever so slightly into the several streams of your thoughts until he can find an anchor somewhere in your heart to attach his tethers of vanity and plant his seeds of pride.

The challenge that faces a man of God who desires to be used supernaturally, therefore, lies in how to be "meet for the Master's use" (2 Timothy 2:21) and yet keep his ego and self completely invisible. God does not bestow His power on just anybody. He may work through anybody, but He is careful to whom He entrusts

His power. We must be careful that our desire to be used by God is not rooted in our self-image or desire for position in God, but entirely upon the promotion of the kingdom of God. As 1st Corinthians 13 tells us, you can have the faith to move mountains, but if you do not have charity, it is worth nothing.

Easily said; not so easily done. Any fool can spout off religious platitudes that boast of unearned righteousness and spirituality, but it is an entirely different matter to fight your way through the spiritual swamp of ego and pride to arrive at that place where God can use you.

I often hear young Christians naively spout off that they have been called to be a prophet. My first response is to tell them to pray and beg God to change His mind and to please choose someone else because you will die a thousand deaths before you enter into that calling.

Ego, pride, and self-awareness must be burned out of you before you are ready to enter into that place of real power. God will give it to you in pieces – just enough to lift you up so He can break you down again. Line upon line, one step at a time, until you gradually become empty of self. Jacob had his 21 years under Laban, Joseph his 13 years in prison, and Moses his 40 years in the desert, and you will have your place of cauterizing fire to take the "you" out of you so God can fill you with Himself. His goal is not to change you, but to kill you. You are to be purified into transparent glass so that when people look at you, it is not you that they see, but the fire of God that is in you.

And so with the power that works through you, there is a deep innate understanding that it is not you but God who is working through you to do these miracles. You are nothing but dust and ashes; you don't even own the breath in your body. You are dead in Christ, crucified to the world, numb to pride and arrogance. Any place that Satan could have gotten hold of has been broken away. You have finally surrendered to God.

When you are no longer mindful about yourself or your spiritual place in God – when you just simply do not care anymore – then you are finally "meet for the Master's use" and ready to wield the power of God so that He, and He alone, will get the glory.

Revival does not come through any other path. There is a price to pay for a true revival, and it is higher than human flesh wants to pay. God will work in those who are willing vessels to bring about great moves of God. We just have to be willing to surrender all and yield to the great Will of God.

For it is God which worketh in you both to will and to do of his good pleasure. (Philippians 2:13)

About the Author

Dalen Garris has been in ministry since the Jesus Movement in California in 1970. In 1997, he began a radio broadcast that ultimately spread to dozens of countries, from Israel and Saudi Arabia to Africa and the Philippines. His program, *Fire in the Hole*, was broadcast for several years across North America on the Sky Angel network as the Voice of Jerusalem.

A newspaper column followed, which has been published in local newspapers and Christian magazines in several countries. He has also written over a dozen books and several booklets.

Since 2004, he has been lighting the fires of revival in churches spread across sub-Saharan Africa. Over the course of 17 years, he has preached in over 1,200 churches and has seen hundreds of them set on fire and explode with growth and hundreds of new ones planted across Africa. Hundreds of people have been supernaturally healed during the healing lines that so often sprang up during these revival meetings, and tens of thousands have been saved.

And the fires are still burning.

Because of his work across Africa, Dalen Garris was awarded an honorary Doctorate in 2017 by the Northwestern Christian University of Florida.

Dr. Garris currently lives with Cindy, his wife of 44 years, in Waxahachie and is still heavily involved with churches across Africa. His pressing hope is in seeing this powerful move of God in Africa ignite us here in America. He believes that this upcoming generation will be the Gideon Generation that will usher in this last, great revival that he has preached about for so many years.

If you would like Dr. Garris to speak at your church or organization, please contact us for times and schedules.

Publications

- ## Books:
  (Available at Amazon and at: www.Revivalfre.org/books/)

  Four Steps to Revival

  Fire in the Hole

  The Kenya Diaries

  A Trumpet in Nigeria

  A Scent of Rain

  Into the Heart of Darkness

  Fire and Rain

  Do You Have Eternal Security?

  Standing in the Gap – True and False Prophets

  Revival Campaigns in Africa - 2019

  A Voice in the Wilderness Series:

      vol. 1, Journey Begins

      vol. 2, The Early Years

      vol. 3, Prophet Rising

      vol. 4, Revival in the Wings

      vol. 5, The Sound of an Abundance of Rain

      vol. 6, Watchman, What of the Night?

      Vol. 7, Mud and Heroes

      Vol. 8, Ashes in the Morning

Booklets:

A Volcano in Cape Verde

Tanzania, 2011

Nigeria, 2012

Planting a Seed in Liberia

A Whisper in the Wind

Finishing What We Started

Two Covenants

Calvinism Critiqued

10 Days in Nairobi

A Light in the Bush

- Available free at: www.Revivalfire.org/booklets/

RevivalFire Ministries

PO Box 822
Waxahachie, TX 75168
dale@revivalfire.org

http://RevivalFire.org